W9-BLV-417

Dropping In On...

Philadelphia

Deb Tuttle Nelson

rourkeeducationalmedia.com

Scan for Related Titles
and Teacher Resources

Before Reading:

Building Academic Vocabulary and Background Knowledge

Before reading a book, it is important to tap into what your child or students already know about the topic. This will help them develop their vocabulary, increase their reading comprehension, and make connections across the curriculum.

1. *Look at the cover of the book. What will this book be about?*
2. *What do you already know about the topic?*
3. *Let's study the Table of Contents. What will you learn about in the book's chapters?*
4. *What would you like to learn about this topic? Do you think you might learn about it from this book? Why or why not?*
5. *Use a reading journal to write about your knowledge of this topic. Record what you already know about the topic and what you hope to learn about the topic.*
6. *Read the book.*
7. *In your reading journal, record what you learned about the topic and your response to the book.*
8. *After reading the book complete the activities below.*

Content Area Vocabulary
Read the list. What do these words mean?

centennial
descendants
expansion
graffiti
historic
interactive
mural
produce
replica
sautéed

After Reading:

Comprehension and Extension Activity

After reading the book, work on the following questions with your child or students in order to check their level of reading comprehension and content mastery.

1. *Why was Philadelphia founded? (Summarize)*
2. *Who is known as Philadelphia's "favorite son" and why is he called that? (Infer)*
3. *What influential events in U.S. history happened in the city? (Asking questions)*
4. *What do you find most interesting about Philadelphia's history? (Text to self connection)*
5. *Are sports important to Philadelphia residents? (Asking questions)*

Extension Activity

Philadelphia is home to many famous firsts. Gather items that represent several of them, then place each item in a separate box with a short riddle that describes the event or landmark. Can your classmates guess what each box represents?

Table of Contents

United States

Philadelphia
NY
PA
NJ
OH
WV VA DE
MD

Philadelphia Facts

Founded: 1682
Land area: 134.10 square miles (347.31 square kilometers)
Elevation: 40 feet (12.2 meters) above sea level
Previous names: none
Population: 1.5 million
Average Daytime Temperatures:
winter: 40.8 degrees Fahrenheit (4.9 degrees Celsius)
spring: 62.4 degrees Fahrenheit (16.9 degrees Celsius)
summer: 84.1 degrees Fahrenheit (29 degrees Celsius)
fall: 66.3 degrees Fahrenheit (19.1 degrees Celsius)

Ethnic diversity:
African-American 43.4%
American Indian or Alaska Native .5%
Asian 6.3%
Native Hawaiian or Pacific Islander > .5%
Hispanic or Latino 12.3%
White 36.9%

City Nicknames:
Philly
City of Brotherly Love
The City That Loves You Back
Quaker City
Cradle of Liberty
Birthplace of America

Number of Visitors Annually: 40 million

Pennsylvania

Philadelphia

City of Brotherly Love

More than 1.5 million people live in Philadelphia, Pennsylvania, the fifth largest city in the United States. 40 million tourists visit every year. Philadelphia is known for many important **historic** landmarks and moments in American history.

William Penn (1644–1718), a Quaker, called his journey from England to the New World the "holy experiment."

William Penn founded Pennsylvania as a British colony in 1681, and established the city of Philadelphia in 1682. He wanted Philadelphia to be a place where people of different backgrounds and religions could live together peacefully.

Philadelphia is one of the earliest examples of a planned city. Most of it was built with brick or stone to prevent fires. Penn's plan also included large open spaces for residents.

Philadelphia Notes
Philadelphia was Pennsylvania's first capital. Its name means "city of brotherly love" in Greek.

The first and second Continental Congresses were held in Philadelphia in 1774 and 1775. These meetings were held to establish independence from Britain and organize the American Revolutionary War effort. The second congress produced the Declaration of Independence.

In 1775, the Second Continental Congress voted unanimously to appoint George Washington as commander-in-chief of the Continental Army.

Philadelphia Firsts

In 1682, Philadelphia became the first city in the Western Hemisphere to guarantee religious freedom.

Benjamin Franklin created America's first library, The Library Company of Philadelphia, in 1731.

America's first daily newspaper, *The Philadelphia Packet and Daily Advertiser*, began in Philadelphia in 1784 and continued for 6 years.

Pennsylvania Hospital, the nation's first, was established by Benjamin Franklin and Dr. Thomas Bond in 1751.

Children's Hospital of Philadelphia opened in 1855 as the first American hospital caring only for kids.

On July 1, 1874, America's first zoo opened in Philadelphia. It now shelters more than 1,300 animals.

Philadelphia hosted the country's first Thanksgiving Day parade in 1920.

In 1946, Philadelphia's University of Pennsylvania and the U.S. Army secretly developed the world's first electronic computer. It weighed 27 tons (24.5 metric tons).

Art, Philly Style

Philadelphia is known for its bigger-than-life art all over the city. Walls, building sides, and rooftops are giant canvases waiting for a **mural**. The art started as a plan to stop **graffiti** in 1984. Now the Mural Arts Program includes more than 3,600 works of art.

"We the Youth; City Kids of Philadelphia and New York City" mural by Keith Haring is located in South Philadelphia.

Philadelphia Notes
The Mural Arts Program is the largest community-based public art program in the United States.

It takes about two months to complete one mural, and they cost about $20,000 each.

Julian Abele (1881-1950) said the ancient temples he saw while touring Greece inspired the museum design.

The Philadelphia Museum of Art was originally built as part of the nation's **centennial** celebration in 1876. The gallery soon grew too large for its space. The current building opened in 1928 and is the third largest art museum in the U.S. Its chief designer, Julian Abele, was the first African-American graduate of the University of Pennsylvania's school of architecture.

While at the museum, people love to act out a famous scene from the 1976 movie *Rocky*. Every day, tourists run up the museum's 97 steps. At the top, they raise their hands in the air like the boxer from the film and have someone snap their picture.

Philadelphia Notes
One of Philadelphia's most famous pieces of public art is a *Rocky* statue donated to the city by the film's star, Sylvester Stallone.

Sports of All Sorts

Sports are wildly popular in Philadelphia. The city is home to five professional teams.

The Eagles of the National Football League kick off their home games at Lincoln Financial Field. Their first year as a team was 1933. Back then, their helmets were made of leather.

The current attendance record for soccer in Philadelphia is 68,396. It was set at the Manchester United-Barcelona friendly that christened the Lincoln Field in 2003.

The Phillie Phanatic is the most popular professional sports mascot in the country.

The Phillies play at Citizen's Bank Park. The Major League Baseball team came to Philadelphia in 1883. The Phillies have the longest continuously used name for one team in the same town in all of professional sports.

Allen Iverson (3) of the NBA's 76ers puts up a shot in the first quarter of a home game.

The National Basketball Association's 76ers tip off on their home court at an arena called The Center. The team came to Philadelphia in 1963.

The Philadelphia Union play at PPL Park, a stadium built for professional soccer. Their first game was in 2010.

The National Hockey League's Flyers face off at home in the Wells Fargo Center. The team first hit the ice in Philadelphia in 1967 as part of the NHL's **expansion**. They won their division in their first season and went on to become the first expansion team to win the Stanley Cup in 1974.

Philadelphia Flyers defender Kimmo Timonen (44) controls the puck during an NHL game.

Let Freedom Ring

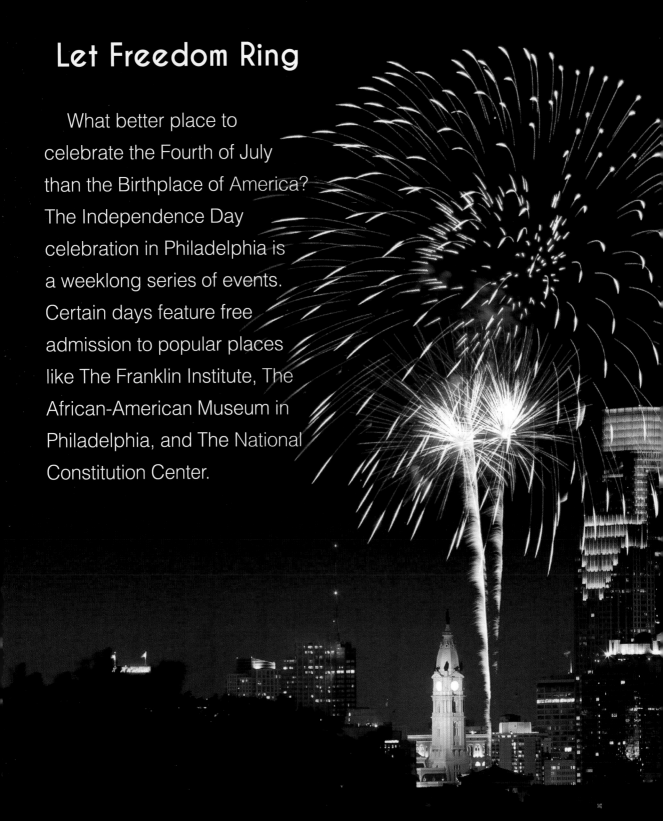

What better place to celebrate the Fourth of July than the Birthplace of America? The Independence Day celebration in Philadelphia is a weeklong series of events. Certain days feature free admission to popular places like The Franklin Institute, The African-American Museum in Philadelphia, and The National Constitution Center.

The day is capped off as fireworks over the Museum of Art light up the sky.

The street party on Benjamin Franklin Parkway is an all-day event on July 4th with food, artists, and **interactive** displays. In the evening, Philadelphia hosts the largest free concert in the country.

Each year, 6,000 people march in a two-hour Independence Day parade. In the afternoon, **descendants** of the men who signed the Declaration of Independence gather to tap the Normandy Bell in a special ceremony called Let Freedom Ring. This bell is an exact **replica** of the Liberty Bell.

Teen descendants of the signers of the Declaration of Independence tap the Normandy Bell during a July 4 ceremony.

The Liberty Bell

The original Liberty Bell, made in England, cracked the first time it was rung. Philadelphians John Pass and John Stow melted it down and made a new one in 1753. U.S. leaders rang the bell for important events. When a small crack appeared, metal workers tried to fix it by making the crack wider.

Philadelphia Notes
The Liberty Bell was rung for the last time on George Washington's birthday, February 22, 1846.

The bell is now housed at Liberty Bell Center, a pavilion built in 2003 to showcase America's symbol of freedom.

It took more than 20 years to complete construction of the Pennsylvania State House, now known as Independence Hall.

Around the Fourth of July holiday, many people visit Independence Hall, where America's most important documents were debated and signed. Colonial leaders met there to discuss Thomas Jefferson's first draft of the Declaration of Independence.

In 1787 they met there again to sign the Constitution and create a better form of government for the new nation.

Fantastic Franklin

Although he was born in Boston, Massachusetts, Benjamin Franklin is often called Philadelphia's "favorite son." He invented the fire engine, bi-focal glasses, the Franklin Stove, and the lightning rod, but he never used his creations to make money.

Benjamin Franklin was the only person to sign the four most important documents in American history: the Declaration of Independence, the Constitution, the Treaty of Alliance with France, and the Treaty of Peace with Great Britain.

Thomas Jefferson, Benjamin Franklin, and John Adams meet at Jefferson's lodgings, on the corner of Seventh and High (Market) streets in Philadelphia, to review a draft of the Declaration of Independence.

Philadelphia Notes
Benjamin Franklin (1706-1790) established America's first hospital, library, and fire department, and the University of Pennsylvania in Philadelphia.

Famous Philly Foods

Pat Olivieri invented the world-famous Philadelphia Cheesesteak in the 1930s at the hot dog stand he owned with his brother Harry. One day, they decided they wanted something different for lunch. Harry went to the store and bought some steak. Pat sliced it into thin strips, cooked it on his hot dog grill, and put it on an Italian roll.

A Philadelphia Cheesesteak includes sliced, **sautéed** ribeye beef served on a long roll. Popular toppings include cooked onions, peppers, sautéed mushrooms, and cheese.

24

A cab driver smelled the meat cooking and asked to try one. After a few bites, the cab driver said, "Forget the hot dogs! You should sell these!" After that, the brothers sold steak sandwiches from their stand. They opened the first cheesesteak restaurant called Pat's King of Steaks in 1940.

Philadelphia Notes
The city hosted its first ever Cheesesteak Festival in 2015.

Philadelphia is serious about its famous sandwich. Dozens of shops in town serve them. There is even a special way to order a cheesesteak. People who do it wrong can be sent to the back of the line at Pat's!

First the cashier needs to know the number of cheesesteaks you want. Second, the type of cheese. Third, they need to know if you want sautéed onions or not. The trick is to do this using the fewest number of words possible. Philadelphians can usually order in three words.

Every year in May, the Italian Market hosts a two-day festival that brings thousands of people to the area.

Philadelphia's Italian Market is America's oldest and largest outdoor market. Vendors sell **produce**, meat, flowers, desserts, pastas, seafood, and cheeses.

The area also includes some of the city's best Italian restaurants, and places that feature food from Mexico, Vietnam, Korea and China. At the end of the Market area sit the two most famous Philadelphia Cheesesteak restaurants in the world.

Philadelphia is also home to a slushie-type frozen drink called water ice. It's known in other places as Italian ice. Locals claim it is better than any frozen treat in the world. Philadelphians are also big fans of their hometown brand of sweet snacks called Tastykakes.

Timeline

1681
William Penn founds the colony of Pennsylvania.

1682
Philadelphia is established as capital of Pennsylvania.

1701
Philadelphia officially receives its charter as a city.

1723
Benjamin Franklin comes to Philadelphia. He is 17 years old.

1732
Construction begins on Pennsylvania State House (later called Independence Hall).

1744
Franklin founds America's first fire insurance company.

1751
First version of Liberty Bell ordered from England.

1753
Original bell cracks the first time it is rung.

1774
First Continental Congress meets at Independence Hall.

1775
George Washington is appointed commander-in-chief in Independence Hall.

1776
Thomas Jefferson writes Declaration of Independence.

1777
British forces occupy Philadelphia.

1778
British Army leaves Philadelphia.

1787
Constitution is debated and accepted in Independence Hall.

1790-1800
Philadelphia serves as the capital of the United States while Washington D.C., is being constructed.

1946
World's first computer is built in Philadelphia.

1987
One Liberty Place is built, making it the first building allowed to be taller than City Hall.

2009
President-elect Barack Obama and Vice-President elect Joe Biden begin their history-making train trip to their inauguration at Philadelphia's Penn Station.

2015
Pope Francis visits Philadelphia and speaks at Independence Hall.

Glossary

centennial (sen-TEN-ee-uhl): the 100th year celebration of an event

descendants (di-SEND-uhnts): a later generation of the same family

expansion (ek-SPAN-shuhn): to increase in size

graffiti (gruh-FEE-tee): pictures drawn or words written on the walls, buildings, subway cars or on other surfaces

historic (hi-STOR-ik): famous or important in history

interactive (in-tur-AK-tiv): allowing a user to control or make changes

mural (myu-ruhl): a painting on a wall

produce (PRO-doos): things that are grown for eating, especially fruits and vegetables

replica (REP-luh-kuh): a copy of something

sautéed (saw-TAYD): food that has been fried in a little bit of fat or butter

Index

Show What You Know

1. Why is the Declaration of Independence important to American history?
2. What motivated William Penn to found Philadelphia?
3. What happened to the original Liberty Bell?
4. Why was the Mural Arts Program started?
5. Name three things that happened in Philadelphia before they happened anywhere else.

Websites to Visit

www.visitphilly.com

www.libertyskids.org

www.50states.com/facts/pennsylvania

About the Author

Deb Tuttle Nelson runs an elementary school library in the town where she grew up. The American Revolution and the Civil War era were her favorite topics to study when she was a child. Her hobbies include writing poetry and music as well as playing guitar and drums. She enjoys coaching her sons in DestiNation Imagination, a children's creative problem solving competition and, of course, reading. A 1989 graduate of Ohio University, she lives with her husband and three boys in Centerville, Ohio.

Meet The Author!
www.meetREMauthors.com

www.rourkeeducationalmedia.com

PHOTO CREDITS: Cover: © travelif, aimintang, Christian Corolla, David Sucsy; Title Page, Page 21, 25, 27, 29: © f11photo; Page 4: © Jeff Biglanl Page 5, 29: © Linda Steward; Page 6: © tupungato; Page 7, 8, 9, 23, 29: © Library of Congress; Page 9, 29: © Wikipedia - U.S. Army; Page 10: © andipantz; Page 11: © aimintang; Page 12: © Olivier Le Quienec; Page 13: © code6d; Page 14: © Anna Bryukhanova; Page 15: © Ffooter; Page 16: © Swa1959; Page 17: © photosthatrock; Page 18: © Tongshan; Page 19: © Naaman Abreu; Page 20: © COKE WHITWORTH - AP Images; Page 22, 29: © Dibrova; Page 24: © Brent Hokfacker; Page 26: © Lorraine Boogich; Page 28: © BirdoPrey; Page 29: © D.J. McCoy

Edited by: Keli Sipperley

Illustrations by: Caroline Romanet

Cover and interior design by: Jen Thomas

Library of Congress PCN Data

Dropping in on Philadelphia / Deb Tuttle Nelson
  ISBN 978-1-68191-409-1 (hard cover)
  ISBN 978-1-68191-451-0(soft cover)
  ISBN 978-1-68191-489-3 (e-Book)
Library of Congress Control Number: 2015951575

Printed in the United States of America, North Mankato, Minnesota

Also Available as: